GETTING IT TOGETHER

LINKING READING THEORY TO PRACTICE

IAN MORRISON

CONTENTS

INTRODUCTION

Good language and reading programs favor a balanced approach and result in a high degree of success for children. Enthusiasm and commitment from teachers and an exciting range of children's reading materials contribute, in no small way, to this success.

Getting It Together links these proven classroom practices with a consistent theory of the reading process to create a holistic view of the teaching of reading and, ultimately, a belief about how children learn.

Literacy programs need to be seen in a coherent way: not just what works, but *why* it works. This book explores a consistent view of the reading process and shows how decisions made in planning, teaching, and assessment need to be reflected in this view. It shows that holding a specific view of the process forces us to reconsider, among other things, how we group children for instruction, how we use assessment to further learning, and how we gauge and subsequently promote comprehension.

1. THE READING PROCESS

The great debate about how children learn to read, whether by straight decoding or considering what the child brings to the task, has been going on for a long time and doesn't appear to be going away. On the surface, each argument is persuasive. However, there is a great danger of labeling all of it "theory" and of little practical use in the classroom.

In essence, there is *little* difference between theory and practice. A good theory explains what really happens in the classroom, and what really happens in the classroom can help construct a good theory. This book is about precisely that: linking theory and sound practice in a literature-based program.

Making Links

The major themes in a reading program are connected:

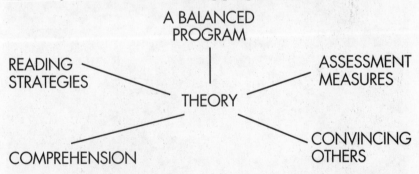

It is increasingly important to be able to do more than just run a good reading program. It is becoming clear that teachers also need to be highly articulate about why they are doing

what they do. In general, theory, practice, and assessment need to be consistent.

Learning to Read

When we pose the question "How do children learn to read?" the answers generated by any group of teachers are thorough and generally combine various theories of the process. These are the more common factors attributed to children's learning:

- They use their language structure.
- They use their background experience.
- They use word and letter knowledge.
- They sound out words.
- They predict.
- They use cues.
- They use the pictures.
- They memorize the text.

Certainly the list goes on, but what is fascinating about the above list is what it expresses about teachers' views on reading. Each item on the list reveals

- a particular view of the reading process
- a method of teaching reading

The Reading Process

Let's deal with the question of learning to read. Once we understand how children learn to read, the issue of how or what to teach becomes much clearer.

INSIDE-OUT? OUTSIDE-IN? BOTTOM-UP? TOP-DOWN? INTERACTIVE?

The various views of the reading process can appear staggering to the point of being unreadable. Any good theory of the process should be able to be read and understood comfortably by the classroom teacher if it is to become the basis for good teaching. Unfortunately, this is not always the case.

Let's outline the major views of the reading process in such a way that we can relate them to what we know about the reading habits of real children in our classrooms.

THE "BOTTOM-UP" OR "OUTSIDE-IN" VIEW

This approach suggests that readers use their knowledge of letters, letter sounds, clusters, and words to decode print and finally get to meaning. This view of the reading process might also suggest that the reader "...plods through the sentence, letter by letter, word by word" (Gough, 1970, p 532). Use of language structure and overall meaning does not take place until after the print has been decoded.

Such a theory has obvious implications for what we teach, how we teach it, the materials we use, and the assessment procedures we employ. For example, letter/sound relationships, single-letter sounds and blends, sight words, drills, and tests of these components become important, as does controlled vocabulary in the texts used.

The process is "bottom-up" because it begins with the smallest units (letters) and works up the scale to the largest unit (overall meaning). It is "outside-in" because it is the outside stimulus (the text) that must be taken in.

THE "TOP-DOWN" OR "INSIDE-OUT" VIEW

This view suggests that reading is actually a "...selective

process. It involves the partial use of available minimal language cues selected from perceptual input on the basis of the reader's expectation" (Goodman, 1970, p 498).

Children use their knowledge of language structure and their view of reality to guess or predict what a word might be. This prediction is checked against the way the word looks. In this view of the process, children are actively searching for the best fit.

Again, this has obvious implications for the way we teach, what we teach, and the materials we use. With this model of the process, teachers will strive to use what is already in children's heads to help them to eliminate words that do not fit the context. They will use predictable text in terms of language structure and meaningful content, and they will assess the process, as opposed to the bits and pieces.

This model is "top-down" because it assumes that children come to the task driven by a search for meaning and gear down to the word, cluster, or letter level only when they need to. It is "inside-out" because it assumes that meaning already lies in the reader's head and must be used to bring meaning to the text.

THE INTERACTIVE APPROACH

As often happens in education, a middle ground is sought. This model assumes that reading is neither top-down nor bottom-up but rather that "...reading is at once a 'perceptual' and a 'cognitive' process" (Rumelhart, 1985, p 722). This approach assumes that children process information from various sources simultaneously.

So How Do Children Learn to Read?

At this stage, one could be forgiven for wondering if we are any closer to answering this question. The answer lies in the match between the theory and what real children do as they read.

How do we explain the following pieces of behavior, all taken from children who are well on the way to reading?

What do I see in the garden?

What do I see in the garden?

My cat $\overset{\underline{is}}{\wedge}$ sleeping.

My cat $\overset{\underline{is}}{\wedge}$ peeping.

That's what I see in the garden.

It's noisy at night when the rain pours.

It's noisy at night $\overset{\underline{when}}{\text{if}}$ the baby cries —

Some shadows s-t-r-e-t-c-h and some just stay still,

And sometimes they $\overset{\underline{scare}}{\text{stalk}}$ you —

and give you a thrill!

In the first example, the child is using her language structure to bring meaning to the text.

In the second example, this child is substituting the same part of speech in order to preserve the flow of the passage.

In the third example, this child has substituted a word that is close enough in meaning to preserve the overall meaning of the text.

10

These are not children with reading difficulties – they are well on the way to becoming proficient readers. In each case, the children are making intelligent guesses based upon language structure and their own view of reality. These are by far the most common types of error seen in high-progress beginning readers.

During the time of dinosaurs

$$\underline{fell} \xleftarrow{\text{SC}}$$

some reptiles even flew through the air! | R

This final example shows a child who uses her sense of the world to make a correction.

Back to Theory

How then do we explain the miscues of these good readers? A purely bottom-up view of the process should show us a different pattern. It should show errors that are very closely associated with the way the word looks.

The errors that these children make fit much more comfortably with both an interactive and a top-down view of the reading process.

What is important about these children's reading behavior are the following points:

- Errors are usually of the same part of speech.
- Errors usually preserve meaning.
- Errors that are not the same part of speech or that bring about a loss of meaning are usually self-corrected.

A Working Model

Here is a proposed model of the reading process. It is only suggested as we can't get inside a child's head to confirm the model. But it does fit nicely with an interactive theory and with observed classroom behavior.

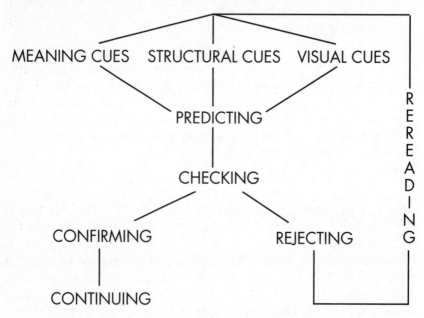

We can see from our theory, and from sensitive classroom observation, that children use various cue sources to make predictions about what the next word could be. They check to see if they have a match, and if not, they reread to pick up more cues. Once they are satisfied, they continue.

Given this view of the reading process, how can we be precise in our assessment of it? That is the subject of Chapter 2, "Using a Running Record Effectively."

2. USING A RUNNING RECORD EFFECTIVELY

Much has been written about taking, scoring, and analyzing running records. However, if a running record is to be used effectively, it must be closely linked to our view of the reading process.

The theme of this chapter is using all of the information in a running record to maximize our understanding of what a child is doing as he or she reads. The discussion will focus upon three increasingly complex levels of analysis: accuracy score, analysis of cues, and analysis of strategies.

The Running Record

A running record of reading behavior is a detailed account of what a child actually does as he or she reads. The teacher accurately records the child's attempts while in the act of reading. The record is then analyzed to determine reading strengths and weaknesses.

Levels of Running Record Analysis

There is wide diversity in this area, ranging from not taking running records (because the children have already learned to read!) to spending tedious hours analyzing every minute detail. In effect, some teachers are confusing process with product. They need ways to get maximum benefit for their time.

First-Level Analysis

At the lower end of the scale, running records are taken on the entire class over various levels of text to determine ability groups. In essence, the teacher looks at the accuracy rates on specifically leveled texts and groups children on this basis.

ASSUMED ADVANTAGES

1. Children of assumed similar ability can be grouped together for instruction.
2. Suitable text can be used with a particular group.
3. Teaching can be geared to the needs of a group.

REAL DISADVANTAGES

1. Present performance doesn't always indicate ability.
2. Children grouped this way can be using very different processing systems.
3. Children tend to remain in their original groups.

Second-Level Analysis

The next step up is to go beyond a simple mathematical calculation and look at cue use. This is a fairly high level of analysis in which the teacher asks questions about why the child made a particular substitution or what led to the correction.

Generally, teachers wish to know the following:

• Did the error make sense?
• Did the error maintain syntax?
• Did the substitution look similar to the right word?

These are excellent questions and can give us good insight into what the child is trying to do. However, without reference back to the reading process, some inappropriate assumptions or practices may result.

THE MAJOR FLAW

The following argument seems logical, yet it misses the point:

<u>woods</u>
The three bears ran through the forest.

Because this child seems to predict words on the basis of meaning and structural cues, intensive work on predicting using visual (graphophonic) cues is required.

If we go back to the working model in Chapter 1, we can see that this child is already predicting quite well. She doesn't need intensive training in looking carefully at words but in picking up just enough information to distinguish *forest* from *woods*. In fact, what this child needs to do is to check her prediction.

This particular teacher accurately takes, scores, and analyzes a running record but has not linked it back to the reading process.

Third-Level Analysis

This is probably the highest and most productive form of analysis. It requires us to go beyond mere cue use and to look closely at reading behaviors and what they mean in terms of our knowledge of the reading process. It requires us to ask not only what cues were being used and what cues were being neglected, but also how the child was using them and whether the child was actively checking on predictions. Did the child reread to confirm or to pick up more information? In short, what strategies was this child using?

When considering a child's needs, we are observing behaviors that may look similar on more than one level of analysis. However, we need to continue to delve until we can identify the significant underlying reasons for the behaviors.

As an example, the following are running records taken on two children in the same reading group. Let's try to perform the three levels of analysis on each to see if we can determine the significant behaviors.

Child 1

Grandpa knits hats.

He knits on the train.

bus
He knits on the buses

↓ *he* R **SC**
and knits on the plane.

↓ _____ - |A| |R
He knits when| |T|he walks

his
the dog down the street.

knits
He knitted his hat

and the socks on his feet.

He knits more than socks

and hats for his head.

knits | **SC** ←
He knitted| the teddy |

R _____
I cuddle in bed.

	E	SC	E	SC
Grandpa knits hats.				
He knits on the train.				
He knits on the buses	1		(m) (s) (v)	
and knits on the plane.		1	(m) (s) v	m s (v)
He knits when the walks	1		m s v	
the dog down the street.	1		(m) (s) v	
He knitted his hat	1		(m) (s) (v)	
and the socks on his feet.				
He knits more than socks				
and hats for his head.				
He knitted the teddy		1	(m) (s) (v)	m (s) v
I cuddle in bed.				
TOTALS:	4	2	5 5 3	0 1 1

16

Child 2

Grandpa knits hats.

He knits on the train.

He knits on the buses

air |**SC**
and knits on the plane̶l̶.

He knits w̶h̶e̶n̶ |**T** he walks

the dog down the street.

He knitted his hat

and the s̶o̶c̶k̶s̶ |**T** on his feet.

He knits m̶o̶r̶e̶ |**T** than socks̶| *his* |**SC**

and hats for his head.

He knitted the teddy

I c̶u̶d̶d̶l̶e̶|**T** in bed.

	E	SC	E	SC
and knits on the plane		1	ⓜ ⓢ v	m s ⓥ
He knits when T he walks	1		m s v	
and the socks T on his feet.	1		m s v	
He knits more T than socks	1		m s v	
		1	ⓜ ⓢ v	m s ⓥ
I cuddle T in bed.	1		m s v	
TOTALS:	**4**	**2**	**2 2 0**	**0 0 2**

17

Level-One Analysis

	CHILD 1	CHILD 2
RUNNING WORDS	56	56
ERRORS	4	4
SELF-CORRECTIONS	2	2
ACCURACY	94-95%	94-95%
SELF-CORRECTION RATE	1:3	1:3

A first-level analysis reveals identical profiles. On the surface, each child displays the same traits. If this is where the analysis ends, then these two children would be grouped together and probably given the same program.

Level-Two Analysis

	ERRORS			SELF-CORRECTIONS		
	(M)	(S)	(V)	(M)	(S)	(V)
CHILD 1	5	5	3		1	1
CHILD 2	2	2	0			2

Level-two analysis looks at cue use. Although there is generally a greater use of cues in the first case, the profiles remain similar. Both children tend to use more meaning and structural cues in their errors and tend to ignore visual cues. Data on self-corrections at this stage is inconclusive.

If this is where the analysis ends, the two children are again characterized in a similar way.

LEVEL-THREE ANALYSIS

It is not until we get into the third level of analysis that the differences in the reading behaviors of the two children become clear.

CHILD 1	CHILD 2
Rereads when a mismatch appears	Doesn't reread
Rereads after being told a word	Doesn't reread
Nearly always predicts when unsure	Doesn't often predict when unsure
Seeks help when necessary	Doesn't seek help when necessary

This is where the analysis becomes important in differentiating between these children. It is clear that they are doing very different things as they read. They need to be treated differently when we think in terms of learning needs and how we as teachers structure our lessons.

These two children are driving different processing systems. They are using different strategies. Chapter 3, "Strategy-Based Teaching," looks at how to use this information in your program.

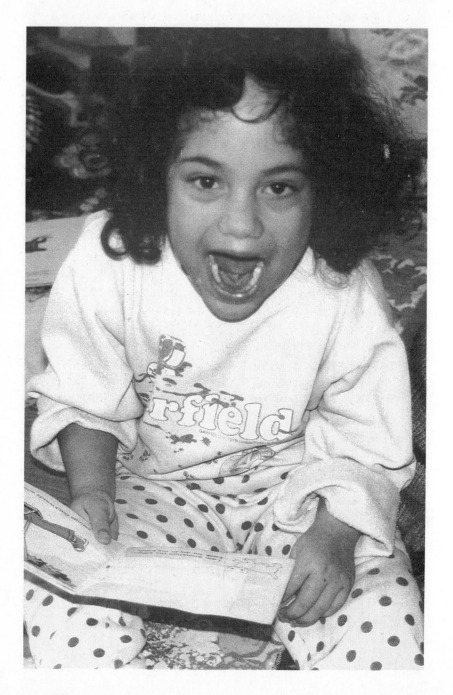

3. STRATEGY-BASED TEACHING

As we saw in the previous chapter, children who are grouped solely on the basis of accuracy levels and cue use can be processing text in quite different ways. This has enormous implications for how we teach. This chapter explores an alternative way of grouping and subsequently teaching children, based upon a third-level analysis of running records.

Before we begin, it may be worthwhile to look at the variables we are dealing with.

Variable One: Text Level

Reading age is by far the most widely used indicator of where a child is in terms of reading. These "ages" are calculated in a number of ways, including noun counts, trialing with children, and other formulas. But any teacher of reading will have been faced with the dilemma that, for a particular child, one book at the "eight-year-old level" is difficult while another is easy.

This is an extremely common occurrence. It is no wonder that teachers become frustrated when working with groups formed solely on reading age. Nor should it be surprising. This is a topic that will be dealt with in some depth in the next two chapters.

Variable Two: Teaching Methods

The components of a balanced program can be viewed as a continuum:

- reading *to*
- reading *with* (Shared Reading)
- reading *by* (Guided and Independent Reading)

From top to bottom of this continuum, the amount of teacher input decreases as the amount of child processing increases.

Reading lessons tend to be scheduled around these teaching approaches. Each group tends to have Guided and Shared Reading lessons at specific times throughout the week. Often the entire class is involved in the "reading to" time, and often the whole class will also be involved with Shared Reading lessons. Guided Reading lessons, however, are usually done with groups based on reading age.

Variable Three: The Child

The individual child is the most often neglected variable in the classroom. Assumptions are made about group homogeneity, often without reference to what individual children are attempting to do. According to our interactive view of the reading process, any particular child may be attempting, with differing degrees of success, any of the following reading strategies:

- using meaning cues
- using structural cues
- using visual cues
- predicting on the basis of a cue or combination of cues
- checking on the basis of a cue or combination of cues
- rereading to pick up more information
- rereading to maintain meaning
- closely monitoring his or her reading
- reading with fluency
- reading with appropriate phrasing

Combining the Variables

This is where the difficulty often occurs. Teachers find themselves attempting to teach a Guided Reading lesson with a group of children who, although at the same "reading age," are processing print in very different ways. This makes it extremely difficult and often inappropriate to construct lessons that are geared to the learning needs of individual children.

Why the Dilemma?

Working with opposing theories of the reading process gives rise to a dilemma. On the one hand, children are grouped according to reading age, which does not take into consideration the individual differences each child brings to the task. On the other hand, the teacher's task is to foster appropriate reading strategies for a "homogenous" group of children whose needs in reading are diverse.

As long as groups are based upon reading age, this will remain a difficulty.

Strategy-Based Teaching

With the careful use of third-level analysis of running records, the concept of strategy-based teaching becomes exciting and highly appropriate. What is required is a view of the reading process that is strategy based and not reading-age based.

It may be a good idea to think of children applying strategies to the reading process in a spiral fashion. Especially in the first year of reading instruction, different children may display similar strategy use even when their so-called reading ages vary. In essence, the reading age can get in the way of effective teaching.

An Example

	READING AGE	LEVEL 3 PROFILE
Child 1	5.6	Doesn't check
Child 2	5.6	Difficulty predicting from meaning
Child 3	5.6	Doesn't reread
Child 4	6.0	Doesn't reread
Child 5	6.0	Often doesn't check
Child 6	6.0	Predictions often based on visual cues
Child 7	6.6	Checks only with teacher
Child 8	6.6	Predicts and checks well
Child 9	6.6	Rereads only when prompted

Given this sort of profile, it is not surprising that lessons based upon traditional reading-age groupings will be less than satisfactory. At each reading-age level, children are displaying very different behaviors. However, if we look *across* the levels, there are children displaying similar approaches to reading.

Teaching for Strategies

An opportunity exists to group children in a very different

way: according to their third-level profile.

For example, children 1, 5, and 7 tend not to check with the text after making a prediction. Although they have different "reading ages," they in fact form a "strategy-based group." These children need to learn how to search the text further in order to check their predictions. They form a natural group in which the purpose of the lesson can be made clear.

Children 2 and 6 are similar in that they do not display a strong drive for meaning. Child 2 has difficulty making predictions, and child 6 tends to rely heavily on the use of visual cues. These children, and others displaying similar traits, could be grouped, and lessons could be constructed for them that concentrated on searching for meaning.

Obviously, other groupings could be made based on the profiles children display in running records. The exciting possibility of using this approach is in developing groups on the basis of *need* and not on the basis of assumed reading level.

A Minor Problem

One problem that could arise using an approach based upon need is finding material that can be used with a wide range of reading abilities, for example, with different "reading ages."

This should not be a concern if we distinguish between teaching material and individual reading material.

Shared Reading is ideally suited to strategy-based teaching. This approach allows a teacher to use text that is appropriate to a wide range of reading needs and abilities and to concentrate on a particular teaching point.

Children can then practice their newly learned strategies on group material leveled at their "reading age."

The advantages of such an approach are obvious. Teachers are able to mix and match groups as the need arises. Children will continually form different groups based on current performance. There will be no need for a "top" or "bottom" group.

A Major Problem

A very important consideration remains, which can be summed up by a quote from a teacher in a reading difficulties course: "They could read all the words but didn't understand."

The next three chapters will address comprehension: its nature, its assessment, and how to help children comprehend text.

4. THE NATURE OF COMPREHENSION

Comprehension is probably the most confused area in the field of literacy learning. Traditionally, the emphasis has been on the assessment of comprehension, often without a clear view of what was being assessed or a plan for using the results.

We may be forgiven for feeling uncomfortable about the results of "comprehension" tests because we don't always see comprehension in the overall context of the reading process.

"My first inkling that something wasn't quite right was when I was teaching a composite class of ages eleven to thirteen. I was required to issue a battery of assessment measures known as Progressive Achievement Tests and to record the results for future use.

"One of the measures was a listening comprehension test. I was required to read a passage within a specified time frame and then to ask a series of multichoice questions. I got through a couple of passages when I began to wonder why I personally couldn't answer any of the questions myself. I was left with two possibilities:

1. *My own reading level was less than that of an eleven-year-old.*
2. *The concentration upon precise oral reading was greatly inhibiting my retention of material.*

"I disregarded the first and worried about the second. My major concern was that this was precisely what I had been asking children to do: to read a passage aloud while I was taking a running record and then asking a series of questions. Worse still, I had been making decisions about comprehension based upon the results."

The Problem with Comprehension

Although there has been a movement away from the use of informal prose inventories, there is still a tendency to create and use age-graded passages and ask "comprehension" questions after a child has read.

As classroom teachers, we could reasonably be concerned about the validity of such questions. Some children who are quite capable readers might have difficulty with certain questions, while some children who seem to be struggling with reading may have fewer problems. Sometimes, the questions we ask don't seem to discriminate.

For example, a child who can answer only three out of five comprehension questions could be assessed as having sixty percent comprehension. Such a conclusion is misleading and therefore of no use to the teacher in meeting the child's needs.

The key to the problem generally lies in the type of questions being asked. The passages used purport to establish a reading age and measure comprehension. A typical passage concerns a boy who goes to the laundromat to do the laundry. Briefly, he puts in too much laundry detergent, and the machine makes a strange sound. One of the questions asks why the machine did this. Obviously, the answer required is that the boy put too much detergent in the machine. However, the answer is not *solely* dependent upon a reading of the text. Either you come to a reading of this passage knowing how to damage a washing machine or you don't.

If we look at other similar passages, it becomes clear that what is often being measured is not the act of reading, but what the reader is bringing to the task.

A Definition of Comprehension

These problems stem from confusion over the nature of comprehension. Comprehension is an active process occurring *as* we read and not the product of having read.

I can find no better definition of comprehension than that offered by Smith, 1985, p 83:

"Prediction is asking questions—and comprehension is getting these questions answered."

This fits very nicely with the proposed model of the reading process mentioned in the first chapter, in which children are continually predicting and checking upon their predictions as they read.

If comprehension is an active process that occurs while reading, then it is clear that questioning after the fact may only be an indicator of short-term memory and the reader's prior knowledge.

If, for example we look at a familiar work such as *Hamlet*, the play could be understood in various ways, depending on one's perspective. If we were to be asked, after having read the play, a general question as to what it was all about, the answer would be as much a factor of the reader's viewpoint prior to reading as it would be a factor of the content of the text.

Comprehension is concerned as much with what the reader brings to the text as it is with what the reader gets out of the text.

THE READER   **THE TEXT**

COMPREHENSION

Implications

Given this view of comprehension, there are implications for what we teach, how we teach it, how we assess it, and what we do with the results of any assessment. These issues will be explored in the next two chapters.

It is important to highlight the following considerations.

1. Children may be having difficulty understanding a particular passage because of text-related issues:

- Layout may be new.
- Vocabulary may be difficult.
- Sentence structure may be different.

2. Children may be having difficulty understanding a particular passage because of non-text-related issues:

- The overall concept may be foreign to the child.
- The child may lack specific background knowledge or experience.
- The child's cultural perspective may differ from that of the author, the teacher, or other readers.

When making statements about comprehension, it is critical that we consider the above issues. There are also various combinations and permutations of these factors that are just as important. What the child brings to the text in terms of prior knowledge and experience is vital. In short, the child's view of reality is critical to reading. That is why any program based solely on reading-age levels is going to experience problems.

Children bring a wide range of "baggage" to the reading task, and it is important to recognize this and make it a prime consideration when considering instructional approaches.

A Final Note

Teachers may want to consider the following questions when designing a tool for measuring comprehension:

- What is being assessed?
- What is the purpose of the assessment?
- How will the results of the assessment be used to change the teaching program?

If comprehension is seen in a traditional way, as product rather than process, then the answers are as follows:

- What is really being assessed is short-term memory and the reader's prior knowledge.
- The often-stated purpose of the assessment is to ascertain if the child understood the text. However, the traditional measure of comprehension will often not result in such information.
- A major problem is that the results are more often used to assess the level at which the child should be working rather than to refocus the teaching program.

In summary, assessing comprehension as a product is an attempt to quantify a process that by its very nature cannot be quantified. Too often, the results of assessing comprehension are used simply to regroup the children.

What we need to change is the way in which we view comprehension. How can it be more reliably assessed? How can we use assessment to bring about changes in teaching programs to allow us to foster greater understanding of text?

Chapters 5 and 6, "Promoting Comprehension" and "Assessing Comprehension," deal with these questions.

5. PROMOTING COMPREHENSION

In keeping with the argument that comprehension is getting one's own questions answered, the notion of "teaching" comprehension per se is problematical. In many ways, a teacher can only really promote comprehension.

Promotion and assessment of comprehension are dealt with in separate chapters because of the need to distinguish clearly between activities that promote and those that assess. Sometimes, the distinction between the two is not always clear.

Certainly, there are some very good exercises and techniques that children can engage in to help foster a broader understanding of a piece of text. An equally useful way of helping children with comprehension is to put into place conditions that will allow them to understand.

This chapter will look at these conditions, the effective use of them, and some specific techniques that teachers can employ.

Stumbling Blocks

Stumbling blocks to comprehension can lie within the program, the text, the child, or any combination of these. It can be a useful exercise for a group of teachers to analyze a story for elements that could make the text difficult to read and understand, in terms of the following:

- structural features of the text
- vocabulary
- prior knowledge or experience

Often teachers discover that the possible difficulties have

more to do with what children are bringing to the text than with the text itself.

As an example of the kind of search one could do, consider the following excerpt from *Jack de Pert at the Supermarket* (Carolyn Heke, The Wright Group, 1993):

> Jack de Pert went to the supermarket
> with his Dad.
>
> "Did you bring the shopping list, Dad?"
> asked Jack de Pert.
> "No," said Dad.
> "Don't worry," said Jack de Pert.
> "I know what to get."
>
> They got a shopping cart.
> "What do you think we need?" asked Dad.
> "Well," said Jack de Pert,
> "we need some lettuce."
>
> "What else do we need?" asked Dad.
> "Well," said Jack de Pert,
> "we need some tomatoes."
>
> They went past the dairy case.
> "Do we need anything here?" asked Dad.
> "Well," said Jack de Pert,
> "we need some butter."

The story continues until the characters have all the items they need. Then it concludes:

> "Jack," said Dad.
> "Yes?" said Jack de Pert.
> "If we have lettuce, tomatoes, butter,
> cheese, buns, and beef patties,
> then we have everything we need to make
> hamburgers for our dinner."
>
> "What a good idea!" said Jack de Pert.
> "Why didn't I think of that?"

They got in the car ...

and went home to make hamburgers.

Let's look at possible stumbling blocks teachers might find in their analysis of this text.

STRUCTURAL FEATURES

Generally, the layout of the text is consistent throughout. But there are some instances that could throw children if the teacher is not aware of them. For example, the text is always at the bottom of the page until page eight. On page eight, the text arrangement changes so that some text is at the top as well as the bottom of the page.

The splitting of Jack's speech (*"Well," said Jack de Pert, "we need some tomatoes."*) may be new to some children.

The use of ellipsis points to indicate time passing (*They got in the car...*) may need to be explored. And finally, page eleven, starting in the middle of a sentence could be novel.

This is not to say that unusual structures should in any way be controlled. On the contrary, these are literary devices that enhance the text. The point here is that teachers need to be aware that such subtle structural features can affect the reading, and ultimately the understanding, of a passage or story.

VOCABULARY

Traditionally, we have searched for words that may be difficult. Often, the criteria for determining the difficulty of a word has been its length, its shape, or even its accessibility to analysis in term of phonics.

Given our working model, the kinds of words that are going

to be difficult are those not already in the child's head. For example, the word *dairy* will be a very difficult word for a child who knows this part of the supermarket as the milk section.

In other words, some children will have a lot of difficulty in predicting *dairy* if they have never heard of a dairy case.

Moreover, no amount of sounding out of words that are not already known to the readers will get them any closer to the meaning.

PRIOR KNOWLEDGE OR EXPERIENCE

Throughout this book, it has been argued that prediction and checking are central to effective reading. Any prediction is, of necessity, based upon prior experience. What often makes a book difficult for a particular child is the prior knowledge required to make appropriate predictions.

For example, a desirable set of preconditions for reading *Jack de Pert at the Supermarket* would include

* having shopped in a supermarket
* being aware of, or having followed, recipes
* knowing the ingredients of hamburgers

These conditions are often taken for granted. But some children's sole knowledge of hamburgers may come from a fast-food restaurant. They may have never seen a hamburger prepared and might have great difficulty listing the ingredients.

Creating Favorable Conditions for Comprehension

We will continue using *Jack de Pert at the Supermarket* to show one way a teacher could set up conditions that facilitate a better understanding of the text.

STRUCTURAL FEATURES

Shared Reading is ideal for structural analysis. It isn't necessary to dwell upon the critical features, but as part of sharing the book, a teacher can point out how speech is used, that three dots imply time passing and connect to the final page, and that the word *and* on the final page doesn't start a sentence but is tied to the preceding page.

VOCABULARY

This can be dealt with in a number of ways. The teacher may choose to discuss potentially unfamiliar words such as *dairy* and *bakery* during the same Shared Reading, or these words may be introduced through a related story that also deals with supermarkets. The teacher may also display pictures or use any number of other teaching strategies. The goal will be to introduce vocabulary in a natural way, not to isolate words or have children learn them out of context.

In fact, the teacher may wish not to deal with vocabulary until the difficulty arises, especially if the particular words are not critical to the meaning of the story.

In no way are we talking about the preteaching of words. This would be totally inappropriate. The goal is only to sensitize children to what is coming up.

Prior Knowledge or Experience

There are a number of in-class activities that can help children acquire the prior knowledge necessary for reading this book. Some of these are as follows:

- The group could use recipes to construct real or fanciful meals.
- The group could create their own book about going to the supermarket, using pictures cut from magazines.
- The group could create a story about a similar experience, for example, shopping for hot dogs or the ingredients for a fantastic pizza.
- The children could role-play their own shopping or their own cooking.
- The teacher could use other books that have similar patterns or concepts to help establish the central themes of constructing a meal and shopping at a supermarket. One such book is *The Hungry Giant's Soup* by Joy Cowley.

These are just a few activities. Creative teachers will be able to think of more (and probably better) approaches.

An ideal buildup to reading this text would be to actually make hamburgers as a class or group activity. This would allow children to see firsthand the ingredients and the sequencing of the recipe. Similarly, a visit to the supermarket would be ideal.

Whatever the approach, the goal is to provide the appropriate background knowledge to enable the children to bring meaning to the text.

The example used is pitched at the early reading stage. It would be easy to assume that building background knowledge is not applicable to children in the upper grades. On the contrary, the older children get, the more diverse the life experiences are that they bring to reading. Upper-level teachers need to look carefully at not only elements within the text, but also the prior knowledge that children need to succeed.

Comprehension in General

It would be inappropriate to leave this chapter without mentioning some general techniques and activities that can be used to promote comprehension.

Cairney (1990) suggests a list of some very useful strategies for encouraging comprehension. These include

- collaborative stories in which the children use a wordless picture book to construct an appropriate story
- story frames in which, after reading a story aloud, the teacher provides sentence starters throughout a passage that children complete to create a logical sequence
- literary sociograms in which each character is written within a circle and, with help, the children write a few words on connecting lines that indicate the relationships between the characters

One of the most powerful teaching strategies that Cairney suggests is "sketch to stretch." This involves the teacher reading to the children and stopping when a decision must be made, a secret revealed, or a puzzle unraveled. Children are asked to draw what the item or action may be. This encourages children to reflect upon the story so far and to predict on that basis. This technique also presents a less threatening situation than a purely verbal or written response.

Cairney presents a number of other strategies for fostering comprehension, and his book is extremely useful in this area. A short list of other worthwhile publications in the field of reading comprehension may be found at the end of this book.

Good teachers, however, will come up with their own techniques and strategies to help promote comprehension. The intention here is to stress the need to foster comprehension skills in general and to provide children with the appropriate prior knowledge when dealing with a particular text.

Given that the view of comprehension presented in this book is of an active process, and not a product, one could be forgiven for asking if we can, in fact, ever assess it. We can— but only during the act of reading. Chapter 6, "Assessing Comprehension," explores this very notion.

6. ASSESSING COMPREHENSION

Assessing comprehension is a confusing issue for many teachers. One must know the nature of comprehension to properly assess it. Assessment is confusing because its nature is difficult to grasp. As has already been stated, not only is it impossible to "measure" an essentially nonquantifiable entity, but also, after putting children through an inquisition on their reading, the findings are not used to alter reading instruction. And, perhaps, that is for the best.

Assessing in the Act of Comprehending

If comprehending is making sound predictions and checking them in such a way that there is a consistent "fit," then we need to look at what is happening as the child reads. Two major ways we can assess this are by a careful analysis of running records and by reader response.

A Fourth Level of Running Record Analysis

If we look carefully at our running records, especially the substitutions and the self-corrections, we should be able to make some statement about a child's attempts to bring meaning to the text.

In a strange way, this requires the child to actually make some errors. A running record with a 100% accuracy level may, in fact, be misleading. Some children are excellent decoders of words.

Let's look at a couple of running records to see how this analysis might work.

RUNNING RECORD 1:
OLD TEETH, NEW TEETH

ANALYSIS

	E	SC	E	SC

Dave|**A**|
Dad | |**T** says I have to brush — E: 1 — ⓜ ⓢ ⓥ

✔|**A**|
my| |**T** teeth

before I go to bed at night.

our
He squeezes out the toothpaste — E: 1 — ⓜ ⓢ ⓥ

give
and makes sure I get it right. — E: 1 — ⓜ ⓢ ⓥ

But Gran doesn't have to

brush her teeth.

✔|**A**|
She| |**T** takes them out instead.

judge
She puts them in the water jug — E: 1 — m ⓢ ⓥ

and leaves them by her bed!

TOTALS: E 4 | SC 0 | 3 4 4 |

46

The Analysis

If we look only in terms of cue use, this running record can be misleading. This child is using meaning, structural, and visual cues—but what about comprehension? To find out, we need to look carefully at these behaviors:

- There is a lack of self-correction.
- The child does not make an attempt to search further when meaning breaks down after a substitution.
- The child's checking strategies are with the teacher and not the text.
- After checking with the teacher, the child doesn't reread to confirm or maintain meaning.

These are critical behaviors when we are thinking about comprehension. This is the profile of a child who is not actively monitoring his or her reading. We don't need to ask a series of comprehension questions after the child has read. We know from the behaviors outlined that this child is not bringing meaning to the text.

ANALYSIS

Dad says I have to brush

my teeth

before I go to bed at night.

He squeezes out ↓ all | **R** | **SC** the toothpaste

and makes sure I get it right.

But Gran doesn't have ↓ need | **R** | **SC** to

brush her teeth.

She takes them ↓ her | **R** | **SC** out instead.

She puts them in the water jug ↓ jar | **A** | **R** | **T**

and leaves them by her bed!

	E	SC	E	SC
He squeezes out (all) the toothpaste		1	ⓜ ⓢ v	m s ⓥ
But Gran doesn't have (need) to		1	ⓜ ⓢ v	m s ⓥ
She takes them (her) out instead.		1	ⓜ ⓢ v	m s ⓥ
She puts them in the water jug (jar)	1		ⓜ ⓢ ⓥ	
TOTALS:	1	3	4 4 1	0 0 3

48

Let's look carefully at these behaviors:

- There is a very high level of self-correction.
- Predictions based on the use of meaning and structural cues are checked using visual cues.
- When a self-correction is made, the child returns to the beginning of the line to maintain meaning.
- When helped by the teacher, the child takes the initiative to return to the beginning of the line.
- The only difficulty is not a text difficulty. It is possible that this child had never heard the word *jug* and took the initiative to ask for help.

This is the profile of a child who is actively trying to bring meaning to the text and obviously succeeding. It would be a waste of time to now ask the child a series of questions.

To a large extent, we can use a careful analysis of running records to make an informed decision about comprehension. These are the critical features we should be looking for:

- A self-correction rate of 1:3 or better (one self-correction for every three miscues).
- Substitutions that make sense.
- Checking behaviors that display an attempt to make all cues fit.
- Rereading to maintain or establish meaning.
- Fluency, phrasing, and intonation.

A child who displays the above behaviors is actively processing print and bringing meaning to it, which is the definition of comprehension.

It can be argued that a child could be displaying all the above traits yet not be getting to the overall meaning of the text. Although this may be rare, it is easily overcome.

If we believe there is an overall concept that children should get to, we can pose a question or two *prior* to reading. This gives a purpose for reading.   If we wish children to search for specific information, we should also avoid asking them to read orally. Their lack of response may not be a problem in searching for meaning but one of overly concentrating on the performance.

The child who can read with nearly 100% accuracy but is having trouble bringing meaning to the text also deserves mention. This can be a common occurrence when a child is being asked to read material that is well above his or her chronological age. There is no mystery here as to what is happening. This is a child who is a skilled decoder of words and who isn't old enough to have the vocabulary or the conceptual knowledge necessary to read at this high level. In this instance, it would be pointless to continue to increase

the level of difficulty until the child reached a level where there were enough errors to analyze, because the predictions will be based on the use of visual cues only.

An important question is why we are pushing children to read material at such a high level of difficulty. If there is a good reason, then teachers need to get back to the considerations outlined in the previous chapter and help children bring meaning to the text. If, however, the only reason for this extension is to see how far the children can go, then it is strongly suggested that teachers look to broadening reading at a more appropriate level.

In summary, the combination of a careful analysis of running records and judicial use of questions prior to reading will yield a much more valid and reliable indication of comprehension than any amount of questioning after the fact.

Reader Response

Response is one of those terms now widely used. However we define response, it must be distinguished from doing reading activities. Activities can be characterized by their generality and by the fact that they do not need to be directly related to the text currently being read.

Response is any action directly related to the purpose for reading or brought about as a consequence of reading. It is this direct relationship that separates response from reading activities. Given this definition of response, it is obvious that response can be teacher-directed or child-initiated. If we see reading as readers asking their own questions and getting them answered, then by and large, response will be personal.

RESPONSE AND COMPREHENSION

A more subjective way of looking at comprehension is through reader response. In general terms, a laugh or a cry, a yawn or a squeal will indicate what the reader is bringing to and getting from the text.

What a child chooses to do after reading a book or a story can tell the teacher a lot about the child's interpretation of the text. Often, the response will be a direct and quite obvious reflection of the purpose for reading. For example, a response to reading a recipe is to prepare a meal, to look at another recipe, or to look in the refrigerator for the ingredients. A common response to reading part of a telephone book is to place a call.

When it comes to fictional text, responses will be more varied. Some common responses could include

- writing down one's own personal thoughts and feelings
- sharing the book with others
- innovating upon the text
- writing to the author
- writing a brief synopsis for the class notice board
- finding related material or material by the same author
- creating some artwork

Creative teachers will think of many other exciting responses. Of course, these possibilities need to be modeled first, to be directly linked to the specific text, and as far as possible, to be child-oriented.

One difficulty with response is that not responding may be totally appropriate. As adults, we read for pleasure when we can find the time. Often, when we finish the book, interaction with the text ends.

Apart from the case of nonresponse, a teacher who is sensitive to the responses a child is making can learn a lot about how that child is comprehending text.

By using running records appropriately; asking important questions prior to reading or, better still, helping children to ask good questions; and carefully monitoring and reflecting on a child's response to text, the teacher can build a very useful picture of a child's comprehension.

There is one area left that is crucial to any view of teaching and learning. That is the possible mismatch between school and home. The final chapter deals with ways in which the teacher can ensure maximum understanding from parents as to why reading is being taught in a specific way.

7. SELLING YOUR PROGRAM TO PARENTS

One of the major reasons that reading programs get into difficulty has very little to do with the programs themselves. Rather, it is about the differing perceptions between home and school, not only in what is being taught, but also why.

There may exist an unconscious division between school and home. Teachers sometimes feel threatened, and parents frequently feel inadequate. Often the result is a lack of understanding on the part of both teacher and parent.

This division is more pronounced in some curriculum areas than others and is especially noticeable in reading. Reading is a highly valued subject, and most parents can recall how they were taught to read. This combination can lead to some very definite views on both the process and the reading material being used.

It is critical that teachers and parents are talking the same language when it comes to reading. This can have marvelous consequences in terms of success.

In this final chapter, we explore parent evenings and helping parents to effectively help their own children with reading.

The Parent Evening

It is important to hold the parent evening very early in the school year. The goals of the evening should be to ensure the following:

- Parents are clear about *what* you are doing in the classroom.
- Parents are clear about *why* you are doing it that way.
- Parents are *supportive* of both the "what" and the "why."
- Parents are comfortable and clear about what they can do at home to help.

Some teachers like to get an outside "expert" to speak, but often parents only want to hear about what is going on in their children's classroom from their children's teacher. Here is one suggested format for such an evening.

1. Welcome and introductions.
2. The classroom program.
3. The reading process.
4. Implications for supporting the teaching at home.

The first two items will be unique to the teacher's particular setting. It may be useful to outline some strategies to use when looking at items 3 and 4.

The Reading Process

The goal here is to convince parents that what you are doing is based on sound research and is entirely appropriate to their children. You will probably have quite a wide range of opinion and understanding, and you will need to start from where the parents are.

START FROM WHERE THEY ARE

Have available a wide range of materials, from early phonic-based texts, to "look-say" materials, to the more natural-language texts. Invite parents to browse the materials and to share with the person sitting beside them how they were taught to read, what their teacher stressed, and so on.

You may wish to list some of the parents' responses on the board, although parents may be somewhat reticent at this early stage. Generally, you will find that this walk down memory lane produces some discussion and a lot of laughter.

It is worthwhile to have an overhead transparency showing the progression from phonic-based to natural-language texts. You don't need to belabor the point, and you can also be sure that at least one parent will mention:

"I learned to read by phonics, and it didn't do me any harm!"

The teacher, at this point, needs to be sensitive to the feelings of parents. This parent has a good point. The role of the teacher is to convince that parent and others of the value of what the child brings to the task. One way of going about this is to briefly present excerpts of text used in the past. For example:

"I   am   on   an   ox.
Lo!   it   is   my   ox.
Is   my   ox   to   go   on?
On   ox   on   we   go."

"Go   by   me   as   we   go   on.
He   is   by   me   as   we   go   on.
Is   my   ox   to   go   on   as   we   go   by?
As   I   go   on   my   ox   is   to   go   in."

It can be great fun to read this text orally as a group. When finished, ask the parents what the story was about. Ask them why they are having difficulty remembering particulars. Someone will invariably mention that the story lacks meaning, and if you are lucky, someone else will mention that this isn't the way we speak.

As soon as you hear that, you have established two of the three cue areas you will be referring to later. This is a good opportunity to present some "look-say" material such as the following:

> "Here,   Tip.
>
> Here,   Tip.
>
> Here,   here.
>
> No,   Tip.
>
> Come   here."

This material would, of course, be accompanied by pictures. Here it becomes relatively straightforward explaining to parents that children can now bring some meaning to the text but that the language structure is still not what we would expect to hear.

CONTINUE FROM WHERE THEIR CHILDREN ARE

This is an excellent time to praise parents for the marvelous work they do in preparing their children for reading at school. It is very worthwhile here to point out that parents help their children build up a store of memories and concepts, as well as oral language vocabulary and sentence structure. The key is to stress that we teach reading the way we do in order to capitalize upon the good work parents have already done.

At this stage, a few simple but enjoyable exercises can help bring home the point. The goal is to convince parents that reading involves making predictions based on prior knowledge and syntax.

An Exercise

Once _____ a time, there_____ a big bad wolf who liked_____ go _____ walks in the_____ . One_____ he saw_____ little boy deep in the _____ .

"Little_____ ," he_____ , "Where are your mother_____ _____? Don't you know you should not_____ in_____ _____ without_____ ?"

Have the parents read through this in small groups. As a large group, discuss how they used meaning and language structure to make good predictions. Take some time to discuss the forest/woods/trees possibilities and the fact that the parents would only have needed to see part of the word in order to check.

This is the time to present the model of the process discussed in the first chapter. Go through the exercise again while displaying the model, showing the parents that they are in fact using all of the strategies when they read.

You may need to use other examples or, better still, liken the process of learning to read to that of learning to talk, stressing that parents accepted their children's utterances as an attempt to bring meaning and to use language structure. Parents acted as great teachers, children were praised for the attempt, and the correct model was given. In effect, teachers are just carrying on with this process in reading.

Implications for Supporting the Teaching at Home

Parents also want to know what they can do at home to help their children with reading. I believe that we forfeit one of our most valuable teaching resources when we tell parents that the best they can do is simply listen to their children read—that the actual task of direct instruction is the sole province of the professional.

Parents can be guided to give appropriate feedback to their children as they read. Once parents are convinced that the teacher's view of the reading process is appropriate, you will find them eager and capable teachers. Furthermore, both the teacher and the parents will be working from the same theory.

Parents want general advice and specific teaching strategies. It is important to offer both.

GENERAL ADVICE FOR PARENTS

The following is a list of key points linked to the reading process:

* **Accept where your child is.**
  There is often the temptation to compare reading progress with the neighbor's child or a sibling. We all learn at different rates.

* **Take the pressure off.**
  We are asking children to make predictions based upon the available information. Children will only do this if there is a good chance of success or if it's safe to "fail."

- **Praise where appropriate.**
  Praise the child for making attempts or for seeking help. Even if the attempt he or she is making doesn't lead to the desired response, it is the strategy of trying that is to be encouraged.

- **Keep the material simple.**
  As adults, we rarely go to the library to find the most difficult book we can read. We normally find something we are comfortable with—yet we continue to learn. Learning for children is similar.

- **Allow time for processing.**
  Children often need time to process print. If we jump in too quickly, we run the risk of children sitting back letting us do the work.

- **Relax!**
  If for some reason things are not going well, do something else. A conversation, a walk in the park, or reading to or with a child can be just as useful. The child is still gaining meaning and language structure and learning more about books, book language, and the world in general. These are all important, especially for the beginning reader.

SPECIFIC ADVICE FOR PARENTS

For most parents, the above six points are enough to help them, at this stage of the school year, to interact successfully with their children at home. Some parents, however, will wish to delve more deeply into the process. There are various ways of handling this, but during the parent evening, you could introduce the process of teaching reading. The parents who really wish to take it on will probably be willing to commit some time to be fully trained. There are a number of programs that address this area, but one of the most effective and least complex in terms of jargon is found in McNaughton et al., 1981, and is summarized here.

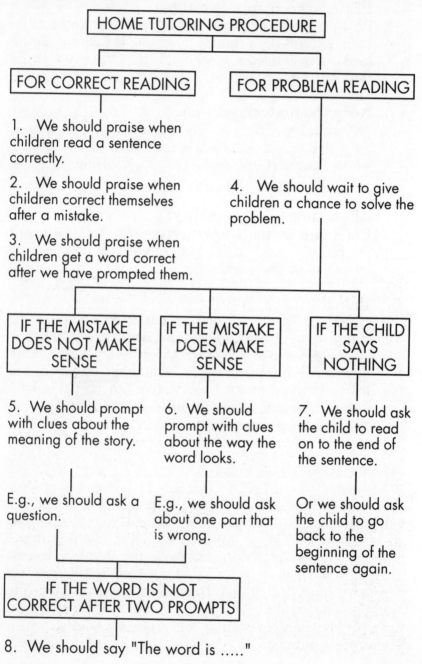

HOME TUTORING PROCEDURE

FOR CORRECT READING

1. We should praise when children read a sentence correctly.

2. We should praise when children correct themselves after a mistake.

3. We should praise when children get a word correct after we have prompted them.

FOR PROBLEM READING

4. We should wait to give children a chance to solve the problem.

IF THE MISTAKE DOES NOT MAKE SENSE

5. We should prompt with clues about the meaning of the story.

E.g., we should ask a question.

IF THE MISTAKE DOES MAKE SENSE

6. We should prompt with clues about the way the word looks.

E.g., we should ask about one part that is wrong.

IF THE CHILD SAYS NOTHING

7. We should ask the child to read on to the end of the sentence.

Or we should ask the child to go back to the beginning of the sentence again.

IF THE WORD IS NOT CORRECT AFTER TWO PROMPTS

8. We should say "The word is ....."

8. CONCLUSION

Education has always been a partnership. Teachers want what is best for the pupils, and parents want what is best for their children. Therefore, it is educationally appropriate that we make every effort to ensure that we are talking the same language and moving in the same direction.

If we, as teachers, get the reading process right, many of the later problems we see with children and reading can be avoided.

9. SUGGESTED READINGS

Resources

Cambourne, Brian and Hazel Brown. *Read and Retell: A Strategy for the Whole-Language/Natural Learning Classroom*. Portsmouth, N.H.: Heinemann Educational Books, Inc., 1989.

Clay, Marie. *Becoming Literate: The Construction of Inner Control*. Portsmouth, N.H.: Heinemann, 1991.

Clay, Marie. *The Early Detection of Reading Difficulties: A Diagnostic Survey with Recovery Procedures*. 3d ed. Portsmouth, N.H.: Heinemann, 1985.

Goodman, Kenneth S. *What's Whole in Whole Language?* Portsmouth, N.H.: Heinemann, 1986.

Guthrie, John T., ed. *Comprehension and Teaching: Research Reviews*. Newark, Del.: International Reading Association, 1981.

Hayhoe, M., and S. Parker, eds. *Reading and Response*. Philadelphia: Open University Press, 1990.

McNaughton, S. *Being Skilled: The Socializations of Learning to Read*. New York: Methuen, 1987.

Meek, M. *Learning to Read*. London, England: Bodley Head, 1982. New Zealand Department of Education. *Reading in the Junior Classes*. New York: Richard C. Owens Publishers, Inc.

Smith, F. *Understanding Reading*. 3d ed. Fort Worth, Tex.: Holt, Rinehart and Winston, 1982.

Children's Texts Used

Cowley, Joy. *The Hungry Giant's Soup*. Bothell, Wash.: The Wright Group, 1993.

Depree, Helen. *What Do I See in the Garden?* Bothell, Wash.: The Wright Group, 1993.

Heke, Carolyn. *Jack de Pert at the Supermarket*. Bothell, Wash.: The Wright Group, 1993.

Iversen, Sandra. *It's Noisy at Night*. Bothell, Wash.: The Wright Group, 1993.

Judkins, Margie. *Grandpa Knits Hats*. Bothell, Wash.: The Wright Group, 1993.

Noonan, Diana. *Old Teeth, New Teeth*. Bothell, Wash.: The Wright Group, 1993.

Stuttard, Marie. *Shadows*. Bothell, Wash.: The Wright Group, 1993.

Walker, Colin. *Every Shape and Size*. Bothell, Wash.: The Wright Group, 1993.

References

Cairney, Trevor H. *Teaching Reading Comprehension: Meaning Makers at Work*. Philadelphia: Open University Press, 1990.

Depree, Helen and Sandra Iversen. *Wonder World: A Balanced Language Program*. Bothell, Wash.: The Wright Group, 1993.

Goodman, Kenneth S. "Reading: A Psycholinguistic Guessing Game." In *Theoretical Models and Processes of Reading*. 2d ed., edited by H. Singer and R. B. Ruddell. Newark, Del.: International Reading Association, 1970.

Gough, P. "One Second of Reading." In *Theoretical Models and Processes of Reading*. 2d ed., edited by H. Singer and R. B. Ruddell. Newark, Del.: International Reading Association, 1970.

McNaughton, S., T. Glynn, and V. Robinson. *Parents as Remedial Reading Tutors: Issues for Home and School*. New Zealand: Council for Educational Research, 1981.

Rumelhart, David E. "Towards an Interactive Model of the Reading Process." In *Theoretical Models and Processes of Reading*. 3d ed. Newark, Del.: International Reading Association, 1985.

Smith, F. *Reading*. 2d ed. Cambridge, United Kingdom: Cambridge University Press, 1985.